Hopeful Tails

Stories of Rescued Pets and Their Forever Families

Photos and Stories by Borders Customers
Compiled by Shelley O'Hara
with special assistance from Julie Bubp

W9-AWV-841

This book is printed on acid-free paper.

Copyright © 2007 by Wiley Publishing, Inc., Hoboken, New Jersey. All rights reserved.

Howell Book House
Published by Wiley Publishing, Inc., Hoboken, New Jersey

No part of this publication may be reproduced, stored in a retrieval system or transmitted in any form or by any means, electronic, mechanical, photocopying, recording, scanning or otherwise, except as permitted under Sections 107 or 108 of the 1976 United States Copyright Act, without either the prior written permission of the Publisher, or authorization through payment of the appropriate per-copy fee to the Copyright Clearance Center, 222 Rosewood Drive, Danvers, MA 01923, (978) 750-8400, fax (978) 646-8600, or on the web at www.copyright.com. Requests to the Publisher for permission should be addressed to the Legal Department, Wiley Publishing, Inc., 10475 Crosspoint Blvd., Indianapolis, IN 46256, (317) 572-3447, fax (317) 572-4355, or online at http://www.wiley.com/go/permissions.

Wiley, the Wiley Publishing logo, Howell Book House, and related trademarks are trademarks or registered trademarks of John Wiley & Sons, Inc. and/or its affiliates. The ASPCA and the ASPCA logo are trademarks of the American Society for the Prevention of Cruelty to Animals. All other trademarks are the property of their respective owners. Wiley Publishing, Inc. is not associated with any product or vendor mentioned in this book.

The publisher and the author make no representations or warranties with respect to the accuracy or completeness of the contents of this work and specifically disclaim all warranties, including without limitation warranties of fitness for a particular purpose. No warranty may be created or extended by sales or promotional materials. The advice and strategies contained herein may not be suitable for every situation. This work is sold with the understanding that the publisher is not engaged in rendering legal, accounting, or other professional services. If professional assistance is required, the services of a competent professional person should be sought. Neither the publisher nor the author shall be liable for damages arising here from. The fact that an organization or Website is referred to in this work as a citation and/or a potential source of further information does not mean that the author or the publisher endorses the information the organization or Website may provide or recommendations it may make. Further, readers should be aware that Internet Websites listed in this work may have changed or disappeared between when this work was written and when it is read.

For general information on our other products and services or to obtain technical support please contact our Customer Care Department within the U.S. at (800) 762-2974, outside the U.S. at (317) 572-3993 or fax (317) 572-4002.

Wiley also publishes its books in a variety of electronic formats. Some content that appears in print may not be available in electronic books. For more information about Wiley products, please visit our web site at www.wiley.com.

Printed in the United States of America

ISBN-13: 978-0-470-17067-0

10   9   8   7   6   5   4   3   2   1

Book design by Erin Zeltner
Cover design by Jose Almaguer
Book production by Wiley Publishing, Inc. Composition Services

WILEY

Table of Contents

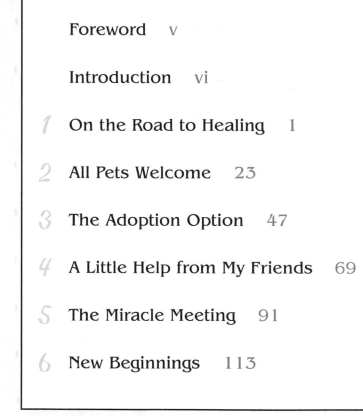

Foreword

I am extremely grateful to Borders and Howell Book House for collaborating on this extraordinary project with the ASPCA® (The American Society for the Prevention of Cruelty to Animals®). Highlighting rescued pets in such an original and emotionally compelling way helps to bring our attention to the overwhelming plight of animal overpopulation and euthanasia in the United States.

Every year millions of companion animals enter animal shelters around the country. Many of them are healthy, playful, and noble creatures who would bring joy to any home. Sadly, approximately 5 to 9 million of these animals (60 percent of dogs and 70 percent of cats) are euthanized every year and never get the chance to do so.

However, some get lucky, and go on to enjoy new lives with a loving family. *Hopeful Tails* tells the stories of some of these pets and the rewarding roles they play in the lives of their "pet parents."

Yet, in a way, it also tells the story of those not quite as fortunate; the ones who do not make it to a home and who, in my 30 plus years in animal welfare, have irrevocably touched my life. For their sake, I hope that reading these stories will encourage you—if you are thinking o bringing a companion animal into your life—to look for a pet at your local shelter. For those of us who have already done so, it will remind us of the wonderful ways in which the pets we love repay us a million times over.

Nowhere is the human-animal bond as clearly demonstrated as in stories of rescued pets finding homes. And the stories you're about to read are no different. They cover the gamut—from tragic to hilarious—and reinforce what the people featured in this book no doubt already know: that bringing a pet into your family almost always changes your life and enriches it in more ways than you could ever imagine.

—*Ed Sayres*
President & CEO, ASPCA

Introduction

In this book, we asked readers to submit stories of rescued and adopted animals, and we were overwhelmed with the response. The number of people who have opened their homes—and their hearts—to these animals is beyond encouraging. We read stories of rescued cats, dogs, rabbits, guinea pigs, birds, turtles, and more. Many of these animals were in need of medical care, or came from an abusive situation, but that didn't stop readers from giving the pet a second chance at life.

People took in pets in a variety of ways. Sometimes a friend or neighbor brought the animal to the person because they were known to take in strays or to be accommodating to hurt or injured or homeless animals. Many readers specifically sought out a rescued pet, visiting local shelters. Some found their

pet online and learned that seeing a picture and reading a description can make a connection in the same way physically meeting a pet can. Meanwhile others desired to rescue a specific breed such as a Doberman or a Beagle and signed up with rescues for these breeds.

Consider the following statistics from the ASPCA:

- About 60 percent of all households in the U.S. have a pet.
- The majority of pets are acquired through friends or family members, but 10 to 20 percent are adopted from shelters and rescues.
- There are about 5,000 independent community animal shelters.
- About 8 to 12 million pets enter animal shelters nationwide. Of these, the majority are euthanized each year because no one claims them.

The facts are staggering, but you can find hope in the following stories and pictures of those lucky animals who beat the odds and found a home because of some welcoming, generous animal lover.

While we couldn't include each of the thousands of entries we received, we know that every one of those pets you welcomed into your home is safe, cherished, and loved. We had fun meeting your furry friends and reading about how you were able to change their lives—and how they changed yours. This book celebrates those connections that happened when pets and pet parents found each other.

On the Road to Healing

The pets featured in this book all lived lives before coming to their forever families. While not all were rescued from dramatic and dire circumstances, others were. For many of these pets, their new pet parent represented the warmth, safety, and health they could have only dreamed of in their former lives. In several instances, had a pet parent not stepped in, the pet may not have lived more than a couple days. The new homes gave these special animals a chance to heal physically and emotionally in a loving home and in the midst of a fabulous and caring new family.

Once a new pet is brought home, miraculous things start happening. The pet immediately, sometimes tentatively, becomes a member of the family. With the acceptance and patience of the new pet parents, the furry or feathered fellas can begin to trust. They can relax without fear of physical harm or hunger. They can be what they were intended to be all along: A best friend, a protector, a playmate always ready to give a kiss and receive a hug.

And the miracles don't stop there. Healing is a two-way process, and in caring for pets, the pet parents receive so much back. Having a purpose in life and a friend who relies on them can give humans the strength to carry on through difficult times. Many pet parents find their pets help them heal from depression, loss of a loved one, or changing life circumstances.

Few bonds are stronger than that between a human and pet who find common ground and unmitigated trust together. This chapter celebrates those bonds.

Schooner was surrendered to a shelter because he was three years old and not housetrained. A medical exam uncovered the problem: multiple bladder stones. Following surgery, Schooner has recovered beautifully, and even earned his Canine Good Citizen Award. Here he's relaxing with his "sibling" Julia.

Photo submitted by Cathleen Luce

Melissa was looking for a friend for her older dog, Ethel. Melissa's husband found Lucy at a local shelter where she was recovering from a car accident. They adopted Lucy right away, and now the dog is healed and has found a best friend in Ethel.

Photo submitted by Melanie Guimond

Jiffy was one of four young kittens dropped off at a local shelter. When Therese met Jiffy, then too young to adopt, she felt an immediate bond with him. When he became old enough for adoption, Therese welcomed him home.

Photo submitted by Therese Todtenbier

After searching Petfinder.com, Amanda found Daisy (left), who had been rescued from a high-kill facility where her euthanasia form had already been signed. Once Amanda adopted Daisy, she found that she is as gentle as a kitten with her Chihuahuas and four cats.

Photo submitted by Amanda Sheets

Sherry volunteered for the Boxer Rescue
and was sent to pick up two Boxers left at
the city shelter; one was Coco. Coco was
shy and tentative, but since Sherry has
adopted her, she's become exuberant
and full of confidence and happiness.

Photo submitted by Sherry J. Insley

Shannah Heals Through Roxie's Love

Shannah Head is familiar with abandoned and rescued animals; she grew up on a farm, full of animals who just showed up at the farm or were given to her family. Her theory is that pet parents don't necessarily "find" their pets; they are found by them.

Once she was on her own, Shannah decided to look for a dog, and came across Roxie, a red Doberman Pinscher mix. She later came to realize that she needed *that* dog at exactly *that* time.

Story and photo submitted by Shannah Head

that every bone in her spine showed, Shannah immediately fell in love.

When she rescued Roxie, Shannah felt she was saving a dog. She had no idea that Roxie would save her. Shortly after bringing Roxie home, Shannah began to experience debilitating depression, spending most of her days in bed. It was Roxie who eventually began to give meaning back to her life.

Their initial meeting could be seen as fated: Shannah received a call from a friend, who was at a pound, totally smitten by Roxie. Unfortunately, the friend wasn't in a position to make a home for Roxie, but she thought Shannah should meet the special dog. Sadly, if Roxie didn't find a home, the dog would be put to sleep the following day.

Shannah wanted to save the dog, but was terrified on her 30-minute drive to the pound the next day. What if she didn't like Roxie? What if there was something wrong with the dog? Shannah didn't need to fear rejecting Roxie. Once she saw Roxie, who was so underweight

Shannah had to get up and let Roxie outside. Then she began taking Roxie for walks. Together they built a new life.

During those initial dark times, Shannah felt cut off from the world, but knew she had Roxie, who relied on her. Through Roxie's devotion to Shannah, Shannah gradually improved. Because Roxie was so friendly with other people, Shannah began to open up. Shannah knows that unconditional love is the only thing that can heal someone; this love is exactly what she got and continues to get from Roxie. Shannah continues to improve every day, due to her own efforts, and in great part to a few nudges (and more) from Roxie.

Mickey was on the verge of death when he walked in the Lawrences back door; they cleaned him up and posted signs. After no one claimed him, the Lawrences adopted him, and it didn't take long for Mickey to settle into his new home.

Photo submitted by William Lawrence

Donna found Gizmo online and adopted him. Donna has been so touched by him, she's even written poetry about how he heals her when she is tired, lonely, or unhappy.

Photo submitted by Donna Blain

Kiki was six weeks old when Tami took her into her home to foster the kitten back to health. As Kiki grew stronger, she also grew right into Tami's heart.

Photo submitted by Tami Quist

Ahna needed a pasture mate for her horse, and she got Paddy Cake from a friend who had rescued her. Although the mini Sicilian Donkey was previously attacked by dogs, once in Ahna's care, Paddy Cake has rested and healed.

Photo submitted by Ahna Fugate

Because there are so many rescue dogs who need a home, Laura couldn't imagine not getting a rescued animal when she wanted a dog. She finds that rescue dogs make the best companions and that holds true for Chok Dee, a two-year-old Thai street dog she adopted.

Photo submitted by Laura Manchester

The Doucettes were dealing with the death of their previous dog when they found Toby on Petfinder.com. Even though Toby has a BB pellet permanently logged in his right hind leg, he manages daily walks, where he gets lots of attention from neighbors.

Photo submitted by Kimberly Doucette

Tiny was spotted near the parking lot of a mall. Aaron had quite the time catching the kitten, most likely because the kitten had a broken leg. Aaron then took Tiny to a vet who offered to put him to sleep, but Aaron paid to have Tiny's leg fixed and fostered him as he recovered.

Photo submitted by Aaron Visnic

Lori found Kramer (left), covered in blood, in the median of the highway. She coaxed him into her car and rushed him to a vet. The vet took care of Kramer's medical issues, and when he was ready, Lori brought him home.

Photo submitted by Lori Hilliard

"Tigger" Proves Herself a Calm Companion

Katie Feltman was considering adopting or fostering a dog to be a companion to her Great Pyrenees, Mister. As a volunteer with Indianapolis Great Pyrenees Rescue (IGPR), Katie heard first-hand about many of these gorgeous dogs who needed to find forever homes. It was at an IGPR event that Katie first learned of Bella, a Great Pyrenees in need of a patient and loving pet parent.

Bella (left in the photo) had lived with her family since she was a puppy. When she was two, her human mom lost a battle with cancer. Overcome with grief and the responsibility of caring for a family alone, Bella's dad had to take her to a shelter—her first of several shelters and several unsuccessful placements. Experiencing severe separation anxiety, Bella was destructive, obstinate, and aggressive. After hearing Bella's story, Katie packed up Mister and drove to Bella's foster house to meet her. One look into Bella's eyes, and Katie agreed to foster her; two months later, Bella was officially adopted into her forever home.

Katie says that not only is Bella a vivacious, jubilant dog, but she seems to have an extra sense about people, which Katie saw when her brother Dan had a massive stroke.

Dan was recovering from his stroke and was living in a rehabilitation center. Slowly he was making improvements every day. Katie was hosting Christmas dinner at her home, and Dan was very excited to leave the facility and celebrate Christmas with his family—and to meet Bella!

Katie was more cautious about the meeting. Bella is a high-energy companion and is nicknamed "Tigger" because she loves to jump on people—often forgetting her enormous size. Katie was

Photo and story submitted by Katie Feltman

worried the dog would inadvertently knock over her recovering brother, but Dan was so looking forward to the meeting she felt she couldn't say no. When he arrived, there was no barking or jumping. Katie kept Bella largely away from the family until dinner was finished; then she brought out the dog.

Bella passed up every person in the room and went straight to Dan. Katie thinks Bella sensed Dan's situation and sensed that he could use some extra attention. Bella greeted Dan very gently, giving him a kiss and then parking herself right next to his side, where she stayed for the rest of the evening.

Katie was amazed to see how Bella had reacted with Dan, so after Christmas she spoke to the rehabilitation center and asked for permission to bring Bella for visits. Each time Bella came to the center, she and Dan sat in harmony. As Katie looks at the big smiles beaming across their human and canine faces, she knows that she was led to the perfect match.

Michele found Scout through Petfinder.com; at the time, Scout needed medical attention. Michele visited him the day she saw him online and adopted him immediately. Today, he is a happy, healthy, and much-loved member of Michele's family.

Photo submitted by Michele Vitali-Daiter

While grieving the death of her hamster and volunteering at the Humane Society, Stephanie got a call from the director of a local shelter, who said that several guinea pigs had been rescued. Stephanie chose to foster and adopt two of them, Turk and JD.

Photo submitted by Stephanie Erschens

While they were fostering Quincy (right) and dealing with his many physical ailments, Phyllis took Quincy to Beaglefest, an annual adoption event held in Chicago. Whenever she saw someone playing with Quincy, Phyllis got a sick feeling, thinking "get away from my dog!" She knew then that she would adopt Quincy and make him part of the family.

Photo submitted by Phyllis Smith

Active in Animal Welfare Association of a local rescue, Michele first fostered and then adopted Buddy. Since then, the pair has joined the St. Louis chapter of Love on a Leash, a pet therapy visitation group. Now Michele and Buddy regularly visit assisted living residences, nursing homes, and schools.

Photo submitted by Michele Swanson

Hunter showed up at Marie's husband's apartment, a soaking wet puppy looking for a home. Marie was stationed in Iraq at the time and warned her husband that they didn't need a big dog. But Hunter stayed, Marie ended her tour of duty, and they're now all one happy family.

Photo submitted by Marie Ledbetter

Cat's Love Changes Pet Parent's Life

Deanne O'Donnell wanted to offer a loving home to an animal who needed her as much as she needed the pet. Deanne had a difficult life, and while she knows she cannot save all unwanted animals, she can make a kingdom for one.

Story and photo submitted by Deanne O'Donnell

After her much-loved cat died, Deanne swore she'd never have another cat, not wanting to again experience the pain of losing someone so loved. But then she realized that she had so much love to give a pet, and by hoarding it she was doing a disservice to her cat's memory. With that realization, she decided to go to the shelter and look at all the lovely cats in need of homes. Deanne could not make up her mind about which cat to adopt, so a volunteer asked to show her a very special kitty. In her arms, the volunteer held a little black cat; she proceeded to tell Deanne the kitty's story.

The cat, Harry, had been left after hours in a box at the shelter. The night was very cold, and the cat was pelted with freezing rain. In the morning, a worker found a cold and soaked cat at the shelter door. Little Harry became sick with an upper respiratory disease and had to be kept separate from the other cats. Because he'd been unable to exercise as a kitten, his legs were crooked and lacked much strength. In addition, his eyes would tear constantly.

While many people aren't interested in a sickly cat, the cat touched Deanne's heart. The volunteer said, "I've shown him to lots of people, but no one seemed interested in him." Deanne responded to the volunteer that she had wept most of her life, so knew what it is like to have eyes that constantly tear. "I'll take him home," Deanne told the volunteer, "and we will heal together."

As Deanne was leaving the shelter, the volunteers from the shelter staff thanked Deanne for choosing and loving Harry. One volunteer said that he knew Harry hadn't been chosen before because he was meant to be with Deanne.

Now he lives like a little king, a real mamma's boy, and Deanne says, "his love has changed my life."

A man brought a tiny kitten to the vet for care, received an estimate for care, left to get more money, and never returned. The kitten had a fractured pelvis and dislocated hip, but an undaunted spirit. Because the man never returned, Christy named the cat Pippin and took him home.

Photo submitted by Christy Moore

Karen volunteered at a shelter and helped walk the dogs. Her husband visited, and Karen showed him Gus, a new arrival. He said "if you want him, let's take him." So they did.

Photo submitted by Karen Harper

Nina and Kita are sibling German Shepherd Dog/Siberian Husky mix puppies who were found roaming farmlands. They were taken in by a rescue organization and found their forever home with Larry, Lesa, Vivian, and Reese Grant.

Photo submitted by Lesa Grant

Emily's friend discovered a tiny newborn kitten who she named Maxine. Emily adopted the little pet. Through continual care, the kitten survived and now goes everywhere with Emily.

Photo submitted by Emily Hiller

Kat answered an ad for free horses and learned that one horse, Sparky, had cancer. Kat vowed to find and fund care for Sparky. With help from Under the Angels' Wings Rescue, she was able to adopt Sparky, who is now the poster horse for the local horse rescue.

Photo submitted by Kat Harrison

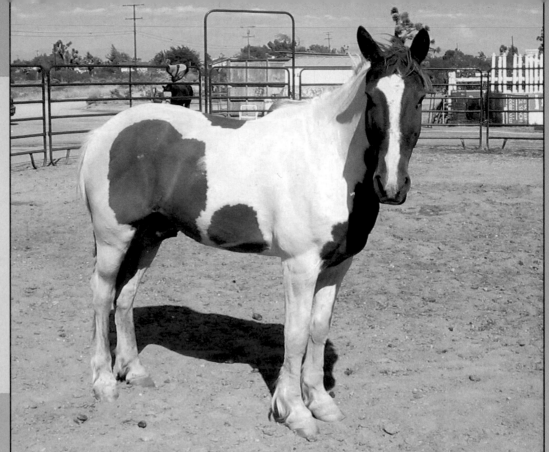

When Erin and her husband were living in the dorms at college, they found Frank hiding in the bushes during a rainstorm. They snuck him into the dorm and cared for him, but knew they had to find a more permanent home. Erin's parents agreed to foster Frank, and then decided to keep him permanently.

Photo submitted by Erin Young

Rose adopted Yama from the Chatham County Animal Rescue in North Carolina. In Yama's previous life, her long, fluffy tail had been broken, but her spirit wasn't. Today she wags her tail constantly to show she is full of joy.

Photo submitted by Rose Stremlau

Tiggerpoo and Ernie both had rocky pasts and now share a bright future. Tiggerpoo was rescued by Clarissa from a local shelter, and Clarissa's son found Ernie after the cat was dumped in a field. Clarissa considers both pets to be her treasures.

Photo submitted by Clarissa Frank

Jennifer rescued Squirt from a shelter. The little cat was later joined by two other cats, Peanut and Snickers. In total Jennifer's home includes two dogs and five cats—all rescue pets.

Photo submitted by Jennifer Bailey

Sady was rescued from an abusive situation and rushed to an emergency vet clinic. Had a representative from a rescue group not stepped in to save her and fund her care, she would have been euthanized. The Drapers found Sady through the Nebraska Boston Terrier Rescue website and are constantly inspired by her courage and resolve.

Photo submitted by Stacey Draper

A Mutual Grief Shared and Overcome

Because Casey and her pet parent, Jennifer Schilling, shared similar circumstances, the two turned out to be a perfect match. Jennifer had lost her pet, Fozzy, from Feline Leukemia and was sure no other cat could replace the love she had for Fozzy. Seeing Jennifer's grief, her husband talked her into visiting a local shelter. Jennifer agreed to go, but only to look.

As she and her husband were walking down a row of double-decker cages, a paw came out and clung onto Jennifer's husband. The cat, named Casey, looked so frantic and scared, says Jennifer, that she decided to learn more about Casey's history.

Jennifer learned that Casey's former pet parent had surrendered her and her brother after learning that he had terminal cancer and feeling he would be unable to care for the cats. The parent had hoped that by placing the cats in a shelter, they might find a new pet parent who

Story and photo submitted by Jennifer Schilling

would give them the loving home they deserved.

Jennifer immediately recognized the synchronicity of the story: Casey had lost her pet parent to cancer, and Jennifer had lost her cat to leukemia. Both Casey and Jennifer were lost and devastated, but Jennifer decided they needed each other to heal, grieve, and love again. In time, both overcame their grief, and they share a special bond that Jennifer hopes will last for many years to come.

When Jennifer gave birth to her daughter, she was worried about how Casey might react. She needn't have worried; the moment the baby came inside the house, Casey became the perfect big sister. Casey still watches over Jennifer's daughter as though the baby were a kitten of her own. Jennifer is sure that as her daughter grows, she and Casey will also share that special bond.

Because of serious health issues, Millie was labeled unadoptable. Despite the label, Harriette adopted her. Estimated to have only a few weeks to live, Millie fought hard to survive. Those few weeks turned into a little over a year, and Millie's spirit was an inspiration to everyone whose path she crossed.

Photo submitted by Harriette Harris-Digney

2 All Pets Welcome

When many people approach a shelter or rescue organization, they do so with a specific pet in mind. Maybe they're looking for a Golden Retriever to help heal the hurt of a recently deceased Golden. Or perhaps they're searching for a small tabby who can cuddle with them and share a common home and some special memories. As many people find, however, predicting the pet who will tug at your heartstrings may not be the one you'd envisioned. She'll be better.

We've read beautiful stories that told of abandoned pets with severe physical challenges who were welcomed into a new home. Other stories relayed prospective adopters heading to a shelter with the intention of welcoming a canine to their home, only to find themselves the proud pet parent of a purring Siamese! It's this openness to whatever opportunity arises and the willingness to take in even the most "unlovable" pets—who turn out to give unconditional love—that makes rescuing a pet such an unpredictable and beautiful experience. As adoptive pet parents told us, all pets are welcome!

And what a wonderful friend to welcome into your home. Pets are joyful animals. They live in the moment and know how to have fun. They enjoy

Margaret went to a pound looking for a Black Lab. Instead, she met Casey, a Siberian Husky, and knew immediately that he would become part of her family.

Photo submitted by Margaret Rushton

being goofy. They revel in helping us forget our troubles, no matter how much trouble they've seen in their lives.

If you haven't already, consider taking a chance and welcoming one of these wonderful creatures into your home. You won't just give a pet a better life; you'll gain a better life.

Susan and her husband found Cricket through a Maltese Rescue organization. Says Susan of their first meeting, "They put in my arms a two-pound, emaciated puppy who really did not look anything like a Maltese, or a dog for that matter. It was love at first sight for me. He was the most beautiful little Maltese I have ever laid eyes on."

Photo submitted by Susan Romary

One day an underweight dog followed Darlene home. She fostered the puppy, who she named Jackie Chan, for six months while looking for his former owner. When the owner couldn't be found, Darlene officially made Jack part of her family.

Photo submitted by Darlene Bevers

Joanie and Pete rescue bunnies. They already had four rabbits when a professor and his wife, who found a bunny while out on a walk, asked Joanie's husband to foster the bunny, named Sunny Bunny. No owners claimed her, so Joanie and Pete welcomed the bunny to their family.

Photo submitted by Joanie Doas

Kelli was born on September 11, 2006, five years after 9/11. Says Susan, whose mom adopted the stray kitten, "Whether she is speeding through the house, leaping on the refrigerator, climbing the curtains, or hiding her many toys under beds and furniture, Kelli has been a source of delight, mischief, and company to mom."

Photo submitted by Susan Rotella

Christine and her boyfriend found
Ema "Duclaw" Itow when looking
for a dog on Petfinder.com.
Christine wrote the following
haiku for Ema:

You're not just a dog

But a reason to rush home

Please know we love you

Photo submitted by Christine Winchak

Xena was rescued from Hurricane Katrina. Just when the Angela and her family were approved for adoption through Illinois Doberman Rescue Plus, Xena was also approved for adoption and joined Angela's family.

Photo submitted by Angela Johnson

Kally and her husband almost didn't adopt Maya because they were afraid she might have health and other issues. The next day they changed their minds. The daily joy Maya brings them affirms that sometimes you have to take a chance and follow your heart.

Photo submitted by Kally Kowalski

All Pets Welcome   **27**

Calendar Dog Inspires Budding Photographer

Jolly, loyal, and tolerant—what more could you ask from a rescued dog? Marie Staddon Dolphin grew up volunteering at a local animal shelter, so she witnessed many wonderful dogs who ended up being put to sleep simply because they couldn't find a home. So when she lost her dog Buttons, she was sad and lonely. And when she considered getting a second pet, she wouldn't consider any option other than rescuing a pet.

This was a difficult time for Marie. Not only was she distraught at losing Buttons, but she was also suffering from mononucleosis and unable to attend her high school classes. Sensing Marie's despair, her mother took Marie to a shelter. There Marie found a cute dog jumping around in the pen. Marie knew that dog, Yogi, was the one for her.

Yogi cheered Marie through her illness. When she returned to school, Marie took a photography class. Gaining photography skills, Marie entered a photo of Yogi in a local calendar contest. Her entry was chosen for the cover of the calendar, and Yogi overnight became a cover dog and local celebrity.

Marie was so inspired by her success and the resulting calendar that she decided someday she would like to photograph a whole calendar featuring rescued and adopted pets. She wanted to show what wonderful pets can be found at shelters and rescue groups.

Ten years later, Marie was living in Los Angeles and working as a set director when she decided to pursue her passion. She created and self published the first Pound Puppies calendar, as well as a line of greeting cards featuring rescued and adopted pets. Her goal was to raise awareness about these wonderful pets, and she felt Yogi was her inspiration. Yogi had changed the path her life would take, and Marie was proud and excited about her photography project.

Yogi, who has since passed away, will always have a special place in Marie's heart for the happiness she brought Marie, as well as for leading her down this special road in life.

Story and photo submitted by Marie Staddon Dolphin

Buddha loves small children and recently saved a one year old from a potentially deadly fall. He saw the child tumbling down a flight of cement steps and rushed over and lay in the child's path to cushion the baby's fall.

Photo submitted by Ann Crumb

Phoenix was severely mistreated by a teenage boy and required care for second- and third-degree burns by a local animal shelter. Once Phoenix's burns were healed, the shelter contacted Marcy, who readily adopted this resilient rabbit.

Photo submitted by Marcy Schaaf

Leeka lingered around Marianne's house. After a few days, Marianne called to the cat, who came, rolled over, and purred. Marianne says the cat chose her family, which includes several other adopted cats.

Photo submitted by Marianne Gray

Magnus was adopted through Carolina Boxer Rescue. With Melissa's care, he became a loving and supportive companion. If Melissa cries, Magnus finds a way to situate his 75-pound body into her lap, and he licks her tears away.

Photo submitted by Melissa Rorrer

Snoopy and Sasha, brother and sister, were found on Petfinder.com and transported via a volunteer pet transport service, which drives a pet from one site to the next until the pet reaches his new home. The two settled into their forever home with Brendan and Kim.

Photo submitted by Kim Santilli-Tommaney

Elaine believes that adopting a rescued animal is the best way to become a pet parent; that's just one reason she adopted Olivia.

Photo submitted by Elaine Contant

Bertram the African Sulcata Tortoise and his long-eared friend, Jack, were both rescued as young babies and brought into Mitzi's home for rehabilitation. Although not exactly raised together, they enjoy each other's company.

Photo submitted by Mitzi Boles

Lisa Finds the Perfect Companion

Lisa Ivy Zographos has adopted all of her cats, and she's found them to be as beautiful, loveable, and intelligent as any purebred. She claims it gives her and her family a good feeling to know that they've helped these animals, and the money they donate goes toward helping even more animals.

One particular cat, Yasou, seemed to have found the Zographos family. The cat was living with her brothers and sisters and mother cat in the parking lot behind the Zographos family's old apartment. From time to time the family would see this young cat with its mother by the dumpster. The Zographos family learned to say hello to the mother in Greek. In Greek, *hello* is *yasou*.

Early on the Zographos family noticed that something was wrong with the young cat, but they figured as long as the mother took care of her, the cat would be okay. One day, though, they saw the cat alone, and she was skittish and confused. When they approached her, they could tell by her movements that she was blind.

They set a trap, caught her, and took her to the emergency vet, where she was given a full physical evaluation. Here they learned that there was no medical way to regain her sight; the cat had a chronic infection in her eyes, and her pupils had fused to her third eyelids. She would always be blind.

Although the family already had three special-need cats, they couldn't refuse Yasou. When she came out to them that day, it was almost as if she'd known—Lisa, too, is legally blind.

Being legally blind and living with a blind cat is an inspiration to Lisa. Yasou joins in with the other cats' play. She climbs and jumps wherever she wants to go and refuses to let her physical condition be a hindrance. The cat's actions remind Lisa that she must do the same in order to enjoy her life to the fullest. She also claims it doesn't hurt to be nuzzled and kept company when she is discouraged.

Lisa is grateful for each day she has with Yasou, and that gratitude seems to be returned.

Story and photo submitted by Lisa Ivy Zographos

Bronwyn was not looking to adopt a new pet, but just happened to be at the Human Society as a volunteer when Tegan was brought in. Within 24 hours of fostering him, she knew she would keep him.

Photo submitted by Bronwyn Stanford

Aspen came from Labs4Rescue. Fortunately, the dog was rescued and put in a foster home until the McCarthys found her and had her transported to their home in Connecticut.

Photo submitted by Susan McCarthy

After weeks of searching on Petfinder.com, Kristen finally found Gretel, a dog who made her grab the phone and call the shelter. Gretel was described as shy, but climbed into Kristen's lap at their first meeting. Kristen knew this little dog had found a home.

Photo submitted by Kristen Bremer

Piggy (a.k.a., Pig Pen) was rescued by Patrice from a shelter. While at the shelter, Piggy helped hundreds of Girl Scouts earn their horsemanship badge. She has also trained many police and firemen on how to handle a horse in emergency situations.

Photo submitted by Patrice Barnes

Pet parent Nancy says Splash, with his winning personality, is an ambassador for the misunderstood Rottweiler breed. Splash is joined by Scooby Doo, a mixed-breed rabbit, who dances on his chubby legs for organic almonds and bananas.

Photo submitted by Nancy Furstinger

Sarah found Sarge, her Boxer, after a long wait and search on a Boxer Rescue website. He was a great comfort to Sarah when her grandfather died; sensing her sadness, Sarge climbed on Sarah's lap and snuggled with her.

Photo submitted by Sarah Auer

Salt was rescued from an abusive situation; when Jessie heard about it, she picked up the kitten with the intention of finding a suitable home. When she saw the pure white bundle, she changed her mind, and brought Salt into her home.

Photo submitted by Jessie Brown

Rescued Dog Is the Life of the Party

Lori Raphan has always assisted with animal rescues; she's even fostered eight puppies in her 300-square foot apartment in Brooklyn, and in the same apartment, she fostered a 100-pound Rottweiler. So naturally when it came to find a pet of her own, she knew it would be a rescued pet.

Lori moved from New York to Alabama and began volunteering with Montgomery County Humane Society. Even though her heart went out to all the animals, one dog, Reese, stood out. When Lori let Reese out of her crate to play outside, the dog had so much energy and was full of fun. But Lori didn't immediately adopt Reese.

A friend told Lori later that she had stopped by the Humane Society and that Reese looked depressed. Lori worried that the dog might be put down, so she decided to foster her. The following week she was scheduled to return home to New York for Thanksgiving, and she left Reese with a friend. The friend mentioned to Lori that if Reese got along with her other dog, she would consider adopting her. While this should have been great news for Lori, it wasn't; she realized that she couldn't bear the thought of living without Reese. The minute the plane touched down, she called the friend and said she had decided to adopt Reese.

Later when Lori was married, Reese was an important part of the wedding. First, she showed up in the engagement pictures. On the wedding day, she spent the morning with the gals in the ladies' bridal suite. Then Reese made an appearance for photos. The florist had made her a beautiful ring of flowers and Lori made her a "diamond" studded leash. She walked down the aisle with Marie's brother and sister. Reese also attempted to get closer to Marie and her fiancé by slithering under the benches towards the bimah.

She then enjoyed the reception, especially since the caterers were fond of her and gave her a plate full of filet mignon! As the night continued, Reese joined the others on the dance floor. The night truly took a lot out of her; she slept almost the entire two days following the event. The newly formed family clearly had one important, four-legged member!

Story and photo submitted by Lori Raphan

Andrea and her husband volunteer at the Idaho Humane Society. She had volunteered to foster cats, and two days later got a call that little Chili had a cold and needed a foster home. Andrea took Chili in, and a month later, adopted her.

Photo submitted by Andrea Foley

Mau Mau hitched a ride for 50 miles underneath a highway-driving travel trailer. After discovering the cat, Cindy spent three weeks leaving out food and coaxing the cat to trust her. Once Mau Mau ventured out, she became a loving part of Cindy's family.

Photo submitted by Cindy Carroll

Harley was found and adopted from an online site. The Alfreds started agility training, and Harley now competes, earning many titles.

Photo submitted by Cheryl Alfred

Bilbo had been passed among many owners, some who mistreated her. Joan heard about the parrot and rescued her, claiming that she is "the sweetest girl."

Photo submitted by Joan Berry

Pamela says of her decision to adopt Bruiser, "I was never the adopter and he the adoptee. We were always equal. We were two souls in need who found friendship and love in each other."

Photo submitted by Pamela Keefe

Angus and Simon were both adopted from the Nashville Humane Association, one year apart.

Photo submitted by Connie McGhee

Suzanne and her husband Noel were driving when Noel spotted an injured cat in the median of a busy road. They turned around and picked up the cat. At the vet, they were asked the cat's name, and Noel replied, "Paco." Once named, the cat became part of the family!

Photo submitted by Suzanne Swafford

Hercules was a stray at Janel's local shelter. He was deemed unadoptable and was scheduled to be euthanized within 48 hours. But Janel saw him and melted as Herc greeted her at his kennel gate with a "high five," letting his charming personality gleam through his rough exterior.

Photo submitted by Janel Greenland

Airport Shindigs Held by Rescued Cat

Missy and James Hatsis have rescued a dog and cat. Leroy was rescued from the storm drain at the airport and serves as the unofficial airport ambassador. (Leroy's story was featured in *Pet Tails.*)

While Leroy is indeed a lucky pet, he isn't the only lucky one. One day Missy and James found a little ball of fur, a minute thing with tiny paws and an injured mouth. This kitty had a plan, it seems, and that plan was to win his way into their hearts. The plan seemed impossible; Missy is allergic to cats, and knew there was no way she could keep the little furball. But Kitty was determined.

Although they couldn't keep the little cat, Missy and James did take him to the vet to have his mouth repaired and to get him a thorough medical examination. They decided to keep him in the crate at their home, but he was very messy, so they began leaving him at the airport.

Leroy, who already had the run of the airport, got along swimmingly with his new airport companion. When Kitty was little, Leroy would gently pick up the tiny cat in his mouth and carry him around. Now that Kitty is older, the two enjoy playing together. Leroy pulls Kitty by his paws and tugs on his back; Kitty retaliates by ambushing Leroy and jumping on his back.

Kitty is smart and uses his cunning to meander wherever he wants in the airport. He slips in and out under the hangar door, and he has parties with some of his friends. One evening Missy had to return to the airport for something, and there in the hangar was Kitty and two of his playmates!

And what a night owl. During the witching hour Kitty is either in the airport hosting his parties, or he slips out of the airport to rouse up more trouble. At any rate, he usually spends the day in his office bed, sleeping off the previous night's adventures.

Miraculously, Kitty has performed his particular form of magic: Missy is no longer allergic to cats.

Story and photo submitted by Missy and James Hatsis

Marti went to the shelter and selected Windy. While initially it seemed Windy was destined to be a biter, classes at a pet store made Windy a personable, trustworthy pet.

Photo submitted by Marti Lorenzen

Sasha Marie was a stray who was brought to a shelter, and then taken for vaccines to the vet clinic where Amy works. Amy melted when she laid eyes on Sasha Marie. She emailed a photo to her husband and, as she says, "the rest is history!"

Photo submitted by Amy Tucker

Mark had a dream he found a dog, so when he spotted Darla as he was walking to his office in downtown Manhattan, he tried to keep walking. He already had two rescued dogs in his tiny apartment! But Darla won out.

Photo submitted by Mark Quigley

3 The Adoption Option

For many, adopting a pet from a shelter, rescue group, or other organization that links up pets with pet parents is the best option for adding a pet to their family. Many pets in shelters come from less-than-ideal circumstances, and the organizations work hard to match up these pets with the best pet parent possible. If you're thinking of adding a pet to your family, check out shelters both in your area and online.

If you're not yet ready for the commitment of caring for a pet, or if your house is already full to the rafters with feathered and furry friends, you can still get involved with these wonderful associations. For example, you can donate money, volunteer on weekends, or sponsor fundraisers. You can also foster pets, providing a temporary home for these pets on their way to their forever families. Be careful, though. It's not uncommon for a foster pet to steal a foster parent's heart and end up permanently in that "temporary" home!

If you are sure you're ready for a pet—or another pet—you have lots of options: the local shelter, local foster groups, online sources, and more. You can also find organizations devoted to saving and placing specific breeds and types of pets, such as German Shepherd Dogs or ferrets.

And while there are "official" adoptions that happen within these organizations, many people submitted stories of an "accidental" adoption. We read countless heartwarming tales in which a pet parent wasn't looking for a companion, but found an abandoned pet on his doorstep or happened upon a wonderful new friend in the most unexpected of places.

People who adopt pets have big hearts. If you're ready to expand your family, keep your heart open to all possibilities; as so many contributors wrote us, the effort of adopting a pet was returned many times over in the unconditional love and joy the pets brought to their home.

Richard adopted Lucky, a Great Dane, from a high-kill shelter. Lucky made himself right at home: These days he sits on the sofa like a human, with his hind quarters on the sofa cushion and his feet on the ground!

Photo submitted by Richard Gunn

47

Vicki rescued Ernie, who was brought to a shelter because he was too "old" and the former owner wanted a puppy. Vicki claims that Ernie not only has the face of a young puppy, but he has the energy and spunk of a much younger fellow too.

Photo submitted by Vicki Holt

Mandy was rescued from a puppy mill and adopted by Annette. Mandy can now run and play in her big backyard in the country; she gets lots of food, treats, love, and warm home-made quilts to sleep on.

Photo submitted by Annette Krueger

Afshan volunteers at a local shelter and also has friends at other shelters in the area. When someone abandoned Charlie, and he was going to be used for research, Afshan quickly offered a foster home. And like many foster parents, Afshan soon decided to adopt Charlie.

Photo submitted by Afshan Adhami

Save the Dalmatians Rescue called Fran with news of a great pet looking for a home. Fran was looking for a dog to become a family member and running partner, and Georgia has proved herself to be both!

Photo submitted by Fran Solomon

Matthew had numerous health problems, but Georgia took on the challenge, rescued him, and put him on the road to recovery.

Photo submitted by Georgia Hall

Deb started looking for a new dog after the death of her beloved pet. While browsing Petfinder.com, she came across Tiki. The dog was in Paris, Illinois, and Deb was in Boston, but she managed with lots of luck and cajoling to get Tiki to her home.

Photo submitted by Deb D'Andrea

From the Rubble of Katrina

After New Orleans was ravaged by Hurricane Katrina in 2005, PAWS Chicago went to the city and brought back hundreds of rescued animals. The rescue was highlighted in the *Chicago Tribune,* which pleaded for people to adopt these needy pets, or to foster the pets until homes could be found.

Christine Hart felt a calling to foster one of these rescued dogs; she didn't even believe that she liked cats, so didn't see a foster cat as a possibility. By the time her number was called, however, many dogs had already found temporary or permanent homes, so the volunteer worker asked if Christine would consider a cat. Because fostering was a temporary situation, she agreed and brought home three beautiful six- to eight-week kittens.

The kittens were tiny, helpless, and sick, so the next day Christine took them to a local animal hospital where they received medicine to combat their upper respiratory infections and injections for hydration. During their treatment, Christine described them as "so trusting and spunky" that she decided right away that she wanted to adopt them.

Her PAWS contact was stunned to learn that Christine wanted to keep all three cats, and her family thought she was crazy. Christine says that overnight she became one of "those people with all the cats."

Now she finds her cats are a constant source of humor and an absolute joy. And she claims even people who don't like cats always change their minds and have a special place for these Katrina-rescued cats, Tom, Moe, and Sebastian.

Photo and story submitted by Christine Hart

Like many foster parents who fall in love with the foster pet, Pat decided to bring Shiloa into her home permanently.

Photo submitted by Pat Thomas

Lori visited her local shelter looking to adopt a cat, but none were available. While she was walking out, one of the staff was cleaning a cage for a cat. The cat, Oliver, jumped into Lori's arms. A half hour later, Lori and Oliver were in the car, heading home for the first time as a family.

Photo submitted by Lori Strongin

Suffering from numerous health problems, Forest was on the border between life and death. But with special care from Elizabeth, he eventually recovered. Today Forest is such a happy, healthy, and spirited bunny that it's hard to believe he was ever a sick little waif in a shelter.

Photo submitted by Elizabeth Huang

Cooper—a.k.a., "Duke"—survived and was rescued from Hurricane Katrina. Michelle saw his picture on Petfinder.com and immediately decided to adopt him. When Duke met Michelle, he jumped up and started kissing her—another case of "love at first sight."

Photo submitted by Michelle Hartwell

Hank spent the first eight months of his life tied to a tree with minimum food and no shelter. The Brinsons rescued him and helped place him in a good home, but he became destructive, longing for the Brinsons. When the Brinsons decided to adopt him, he stopped being destructive and took his place as a member of his new forever family.

Photo submitted by Kathy Brinson

Failing Foster 101

After the death of Willie Sam, their beloved Australian Shepherd/Border Collie mix, Carole and Clint Wade felt they weren't ready for a new pet. Yet, they wanted to do something to help other dogs in Willie Sam's memory, so they volunteered as transport drivers with Aussie Rescue. In this role, they helped move dogs migrating from kill shelters to foster homes. Carole also volunteered to foster a dog, if necessary.

One day Carole received a frantic call from her area rescue representative. The transport driver for a particular area was severely ill, and an Aussie named Hannah was in jeopardy of immediate euthanasia. The rescue staff had fallen in love with her, but the dog had already been at the shelter the allotted 14 days and would be put to sleep that afternoon unless someone picked her up.

Carole readily agreed to drive the four hours to Huntington, West Virginia, to pick up Hannah, who had passed the test for temperament and adoptability. Carole paid the fees, completed the paperwork, and took Hannah home with her.

Carole was immediately touched by Hannah's sad, soulful eyes and what seemed to be her self-defeated attitude. So Carole decided to try her hand at fostering this dog. Carole and Clint made a pact that they would only foster the dog until she had recovered physically and emotionally. But Carole claims, "God had other plans for us."

Aussies are known for their outgoing personalities and high energy levels, but Hannah was reserved and timid. She was hesitant to open up and love or receive love. Carole and Clint wondered what had happened to have taken away this dog's self-esteem.

Initially, Hannah seemed to be overwhelmed by too much touching or closeness, but slowly she began to warm to Clint, resting against his legs or sitting at his feet. Eventually, she began to open up more and more.

Carole knew she had to face the facts: They were now a family. Carole and Clint couldn't betray the trust the dog had struggled to find in herself, and they weren't ready to give her up; they had fallen in love with her. Hannah was their first foster dog, and they adopted her, hence "failing Foster 101."

Hannah has since grown in confidence and affection and now freely gives and accepts love. She has been a terrific foster sister to more than 20 rescued dogs who have come through the Wades' home, helping them teach the foster dogs how to play, where to potty, and how to be good pets.

Through Hannah, the Wades have learned an important lesson. Although they will be hurt when Hannah eventually leaves them, they will be able to love again. They'll find another wonderful rescued dog, and they'll once again know the joys that only these special dogs can bring.

Photo and story submitted by Carole Wade

Kessy saw something special in the eyes of Potts and decided to adopt him. Once home, Kessy says, "it was a dream come true."

Photo submitted by Kessy Stevens

Julia was considering getting a dog when a friend mentioned that Tristan was on the list to be put to sleep. Julia quickly stepped in and adopted him.

Photo submitted by Julia Whalen

Tami did a lot of research on puppy mills, and knew she wanted to save one of their victims. She consequently adopted Max, who she describes as her best friend.

Photo submitted by Tami Marchionda

Mattie was intended to be a companion to Andra's aunt. Once home, they learned Mattie had epilepsy and Andra's aunt couldn't provide the care he needed, so she gave Mattie back to Andra. Andra was delighted, and she and Mattie now share a wonderful bond.

Photo submitted by Andra Shipley

Sheri was looking for a companion for her other cat, so she regularly checked the Atlanta Pet Rescue website. There she saw a picture of Milo and fell in love. He was sick initially, but with some help from the vet and a lot of love, he is now a healthy and happy cat.

Photo submitted by Sheri Budd

Angela was in a grooming shop and saw the technician bathing a very uncooperative dog named Sophie. Angela spoke calmly to the Sophie, who looked Angela in the eye and held her gaze. The groomer told Angela that Sophie was a Humane Society dog up for adoption, and Angela immediately adopted her.

Photo submitted by Angela Cook

Chunky was found in a dumpster at the Arizona Humane Society; Krista discovered him through a local Arizona rescue group and adopted him. Today Chunky sleeps with Krista every night, and Krista falls asleep to the sound of Chunky's purring.

Photo submitted by Krista Fletcher

Joanna found Barney through the Cairn Terrier Club of Sacramento Valley rescue. Barney is a 3½-year cancer survivor who lost his leg to the disease. Joanna is also a survivor of a particularly aggressive cancer, so they were a great match.

Photo submitted by Joanna McGinn

Saving One Pet at a Time

Louise Zbozny is well acquainted with the experience and love of adopting pets. She had Duke, a black Lab, who turned up on her back porch rail-thin and peppered with buckshot. Duke eventually succumbed to an aggressive form of leukemia. After his death, a friend called about a dog found wandering on the highway. Louise accepted this dog, Penny, a beautiful golden dog with sleek fur, liquid eyes, and a streaming, silken tail. Next came Harry, an enormous Old English Sheepdog adopted from the Pittsburgh Old English Sheepdog Rescue.

With so many homeless animals, Louise often feels sad for the pets who aren't saved. When those thoughts arise, she thinks of the advice of Mother Teresa, who was once asked how she thought she could possibly save all the poor of Calcutta. Mother Teresa responded simply, "one can only save one at a time." It's this attitude that led Louise to rescue her long-eared companion.

Driving to work one morning, the Western Pennsylvania Humane Society announced over the radio that they were desperate for adopters for rabbits of all ages. Louise was unaware that local shelters accepted rabbits or that rabbits could be adopted from a shelter. For Louise, who had recently lost a rabbit, the timing was perfect.

Many rabbits were waiting for adoptions, but Louise found herself attracted to a small brown, gray, and white rabbit with two huge unsightly and obviously painful abscesses on his jaw. Instead of retreating to the back of his cage, the rabbit came over to see Louise. He clearly wanted to make a new friend. She asked the workers at the shelter if she could hold him for a while, and the rest, as they say, is history. Oliver now makes his home among his canine siblings.

Photo and story submitted by Louise Zbozny

Louise feels great joy when her dog Harry lopes through the fields or when Oliver attacks a new toy with more zest and gusto. Says Louise of the household of furry friends she hosts, "no amount of money can buy the joy that these animals give us."

Grace was abused by a teenager, and fortunately rescued and taken to a local shelter. Her story appeared in the paper, and several people donated money to go towards her medical needs. Jill met Grace at the shelter, followed her progress, and decided to adopt her.

Photo submitted by Jill Franco

A friend in Jennifer's hometown found Brandy on a cold January day; the kitten had been dumped in a local park. The friend brought the cat home and then set about trying to find a good home for her. When Jennifer received the email with Brandy's picture, she knew that this cat was meant for her family.

Photo submitted by Jennifer Tripp

The weekend that Kelli and her husband eloped, they stopped at Petco to pick up treats for Kelli's husband's dog. A rescue group was stationed outside the store with Harmony, an adorable Black Lab mix female pup. Kelli's husband claims Harmony was their wedding present.

Photo submitted by Kelli Fisher

Ash was found under a garbage dumpster the day Mary and John moved into their apartment. The cat seemed to be asking for a home, so Mary gave her one.

Photo submitted by Mary Duros

Elisabeth went to New Orleans after Katrina to help with animal search and rescue. Elisabeth's first rescue was an American Pit Bull she named Nola. Nola was sweet and loving, and Elisabeth agreed to foster, and then adopt, her.

Photo submitted by Elisabeth Davis

Hunter was one of four Dachschund puppies rescued from a puppy mill by Carrie's mother. By the time little Hunter was old enough to be adopted, Carrie and her children had fallen in love with him, and adopted him themselves.

Photo submitted by Carrie Young

Determined Adoptee Wages the Fight of Her Life

One day the daughters of one of Linda Walkup's friends happened upon Dozer, an American Pit Bull, who was wandering in the streets. The friend had a three-pound male dog, and Dozer and the dog played amicably; they seemed destined to be friends. One fateful day, however, Linda's friend arrived home, the little dog ran to greet her, and Dozer bit the dog. It was clear that Dozer needed to find a new home, and Linda was willing to provide one. After picking up Dozer, Linda bought a bed, kennel, and toys so that he could make himself comfortable in his new environment.

Photo and story submitted by Linda Walkup

But the adoption wasn't going to be so easy. The friend called the next day and said she had called the police with the intent to put Dozer down. Soon a police officer visited Linda and told her that if she didn't relinquish the dog, Dozer would be removed. If Linda wanted to keep Dozer, she was told, she would need to call the Humane Society and get that organization involved in saving the dog.

Thus began the long process of keeping Dozer. Linda began by phoning the Humane Society; the organization sent an animal control officer to her house. Fortunately for Linda and Dozer, the animal control officer was a pet parent to two American Pit Bulls, so he offered to speak to his manager on Dozer's behalf. Linda then spoke with the manager for two hours, pleading her case.

During this process, Dozer stayed at the Humane Society, where he was well cared for but seemed sad and homesick. Linda visited him often during the decision process. Meanwhile, she continued to explain the situation to anyone who would listen, including lawyers, begging that Dozer not be killed.

Another animal control officer visited Linda's house and observed positively that the home had a large backyard and professional dog runs. Finally the call Linda had been waiting for came through: She could pick up Dozer.

Since Linda's battle to save her dog, Dozer has turned out to be an excellent pet and has shown no aggression toward other animals. In fact, Linda laughs that Dozer is scared to death of the family cat!

When Tracy's dog Stevie Ray died, the house felt empty. She began searching for a new dog to welcome home, and found Tucker at a local shelter.

Photo submitted by Tracy Williams

Little Imp was part of a litter birthed by a stray cat who broke into Barbara's basement. When Barbara found the kittens, Little Imp was in extremely poor health and needed medical attention. Three years later, she's healthy and happy in Barbara's home.

Photo submitted by Barbara Cramer

Ellen was visiting her son and saw Buzz living next door, tied up in a fenced yard. The dog was sweet but clearly neglected. Through a lot of negotiation, Ellen and her husband were able to bring Buzz to their home, where he is now fit, happy, and loved.

Photo submitted by Ellen Tish

"A Little Help from My Friends

Rescued pets, more than others, often need some extra help acclimating to their new, secure, loving home. Recovering from physically or emotionally difficult situations may require time, patience, and TLC from the new pet parents, but the return on that emotional investment can be astonishing. This chapter celebrates both the friends who helped these pets adjust to their new homes, as well as the great friends the rescued pets became.

Once pets adjust and are comfortable in their surroundings, they form strong, lasting relationships with their parents and family, as well with their other animal friends. They greet their "people" family with unconditional love, take pleasure in long strolls and brisk runs, and seem to crave quiet time together, kicking back to watch TV or take in a colorful sunset together. They consider themselves an equal member of the family and will let you know if they aren't getting enough attention! In some cases, this loyalty and love extends beyond everyday affection to heroic acts that protect these human parents and siblings.

In addition to the bonds they form with the pet parents, pets also create relationships with other animals in the home. Initially, bringing a new pet into the home may take some adjustment, but it requires only a bit of patience and perseverance to integrate a new sibling into a happy animal

Pamela and her husband found Mimi, abandoned and severely hurt, on the side of the road. They felt they couldn't leave her, so took her in. Pamela claims that Mimi actually rescued her, coming into her life and providing boundless love during an intensely painful period of time.

Photo submitted by Pamela Crouser

family. With time, the pets learn how to share, get along, and enjoy each other's company.

As all pet parents know, friendship with these four-legged, furry, or feathered creatures is a two-way street, with everyone the giver and benefactor of untold benefits.

69

Peaches was part of a pit fighting ring, had been chained outside her whole life, and had been used as a breeding machine. Even so, Peaches has a great temperament. When Patty rescued Peaches, she planned to place her in an adoptive home, but ended up keeping her.

Photo submitted by Patty Letawsky

Marilyn found Maxwell while, on a whim, searching for Italian Greyhounds on Petfinder.com. Although there was no photo of Max, the description won Marilyn over, and she soon adopted the gorgeous dog.

Photo submitted by Marilyn Goldberg

The Bouleys have rescued and adopted two pets: a Siberian Husky, Loki, and a mixed breed, Jesse James. When Jesse had to have a total hip replacement, Loki took over as nurse, lying next to him and protecting him.

Photo submitted by Elizabeth Bouley

Bari debated for weeks about whether to adopt Dottie and Dobie, brother and sister cats who had been together since birth and who were intended to be adopted out as a pair. Finally, Bari's heart won, and the two siblings were brought to their new home.

Photo submitted by Bari Hertz

Chance Proves Himself a True Road Pal

Donna Koga breeds Golden Retrievers and is considering also breeding Newfoundlands. She is a member of a Newfoundland email list, and one day read a story about a Newfoundland and a Golden Retriever in need of a rescue and a home together. Donna immediately called the rescue organization and started the adoption process. Within 24 hours, her husband was on his way from their home in Maryland to Atlanta to pick up the pair.

Photo and story submitted by Donna Koga

When Donna returned home with her new pets she found that the Golden, Lucy, was actually a Toller–Nova Scotia Duck Tolling Retriever—a detail that mattered little to Donna and her husband. They felt that both dogs, Lucy and her Newfoundland friend Chance, were pure gold.

Donna learned of the true level of the dogs' friendship through a story about the pair passed on by the rescue organization.

In their previous home, the two dogs had escaped together, bolting out the door and running off. For several days they were not seen. The original owner put up posters mentioning the two would be traveling as a pair. Finally a call came in from a vet in Atlanta who had custody of the runaways.

The vet conveyed that a gentleman driving on an Atlanta highway had picked up the dogs. The gentleman had witnessed Lucy darting into traffic and getting struck by a car. Chance saw the incident from the roadside, bolted out into traffic, and stood over Lucy in the middle of the highway, blocking her injured body and protecting her from oncoming traffic.

The gentleman stopped and lifted Lucy in the car, and Chance immediately jumped into the car as well. The dogs were taken to a local vet office, and the vet recognized them from a poster. Lucy's injuries included a broken leg, and Chance stayed with her as she healed.

Both are now settled into their new home in Maryland, and Chance continues to watch out for Lucy. In fact, he is boss of all the owner's dogs, watching and correcting anyone who misbehaves. Says Donna about she and her husband "rescuing" Chance and Lucy: "We know that we're the lucky ones!"

Rotar and Beverage were given to Lauren and her husband. One night Rotar got out, and after a frantic search didn't turn up the cat, Lauren's husband got the idea to tape Beverage's meows and play them on a boom box as they drove around the neighborhood. Sure enough, the recordings brought Rotar home.

Photo submitted by Lauren Gunderson

Natasha and her husband found Casey when they were looking for a companion for their other dog, Asia. The dogs turned out to be the best of friends.

Photo submitted by Natasha Villanueva

When he was rescued by a Basset Buddies rescue group, Howard was in horrible shape. He started out as a foster dog with Sara and ended up staying because, Sara claims, he was just too cute to pass up.

Photo submitted by Sara Decker

Leanne rescued both Rugby and Maddie. Rugby began as a foster pet, and Maddie was rescued after being left at a shelter. The two dogs are now perfect companions.

Photo submitted by Leanne Lauber

Phyllis had recently lost a beloved rabbit when a friend spotted Alvin at a rescue website. Phyllis drove the three hours to meet Alvin, and the two fell in love. Amazingly, Alvin roams the house freely with Phyllis's Beagles, all of them getting along wonderfully!

Photo submitted by Phyllis Smith

Lisa found Brody, an American Pit Bull, after her sixth trip to the Humane Society. Despite a multitude of costly health problems, Brody was a joy, and Lisa can't imagine life without him. She now plans to have him certified as a Therapy Dog so that Brody can share his gifts with others.

Photo submitted by Lisa Yates

Amy adopted Patti Smith from a shelter, and the two became best friends. Amy was devastated when Patti, at age four, was diagnosed with cancer. Always the most upbeat and positive of dogs, she amazed the veterinary staff by bestowing kisses and smiles even as they were administering shots or taking out sutures.

Photo submitted by Amy Calmann

Garfield Encourages Rescued Cat

One day when Erika Laguna's husband was taking a break from work, he heard noises coming from a nearby garbage can. He looked inside, unsure of what he would find, but confident that no one would throw away a live animal. As the noises continued, he began taking out items one at a time, finally picking up a milk carton. He opened the carton slowly and to his surprise found a little kitten in need of medical attention.

He brought the cat home, aptly named her Milkbox, and tried bottle feeding her. When she didn't respond to the bottle, he and Erika took Milkbox to the vet. Here they received the disheartening news that the cat had been abused and was suffering from ear mites, fleas, worms, and trauma from the abuse. They started the cat on medicine and watched her night and day until she healed physically and psychologically.

Fortunately, Erika and her husband weren't the only nurses in attendance over Milkbox. The owners' other cat, Garfield, pitched in a paw. Garfield was protective of Milkbox and would sit next to her carrier, keeping her company and providing encouragement on the long road to healing. As a result, Milkbox and Garfield became best friends, and Milkbox has made tremendous physical and emotional progress. Despite her past, she has now begun to trust people again and is willing to give and receive love.

With the help of her pet parent Erika and her feline sibling Garfield, Milkbox will always be loved and taken care of, and will never need to worry about being hurt again.

Photo and story submitted by Erika Laguna

Madison is one of two abandoned puppies that Melissa and her family rescued just before Christmas one year. She describes the mixed dog as spunky and loving.

Photo submitted by Melissa Blakley

Melanie adopted Kona on a happenstance visit to a shelter. On her way out, she noticed a a little black ball of nothing that happened to be the runt of the litter; she adopted this dog, as well. From the runt, Bruiser grew to 85 pounds!

Photo submitted by Melanie Downard

Wendi and her family rescued Maxie, Grace, and Alice. Although it was a slow process, the three cats now get along with Melissa's other pets: two cats (both adopted from shelters), a dog (adopted from the local pound), and two guinea pigs (also adopted from a rescue group).

Photo submitted by Wendi Kast

Heather searched rabbit rescue websites looking for a mate for her rabbit Hopkins. There she discovered Spirit, who came from an abusive past. Spirit and Hopkins met, and after the first few tentative months, are now inseparable.

Photo submitted by Heather Smith

Maria has a huge heart. She found Manchas outside her workplace and took her in; she found Pecas on the road and rescued him. These two dogs joined Maria's other dog, Lester, and they are now one big happy family.

Photo submitted by Maria De la Fuente

Cookie was taken in by Lisa when an elderly neighbor at their previous home couldn't care for her anymore. There Cookie joined the family's other cat, Oreo. Oreo and Cookie love to play and snuggle together.

Photo submitted by Lisa Boehmer

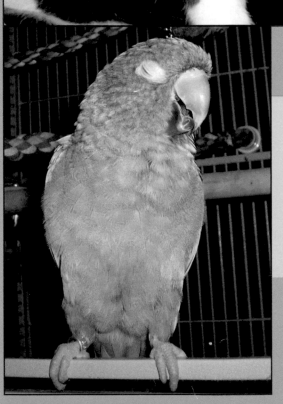

Oscar, a Blue-Crowned Conure, had been residing in a cramped cage with little attention when Melanie rescued him. She lavished loving attention and great food on him, and says it was as if a different bird took his place—one who likes to snuggle and make his friends laugh.

Photo submitted by Melanie Chouinard

Abused Horse Mentors Younger Companion

Mary Beth Hall was dismayed to learn of an abused horse, Copper, who was staked outdoors on a chain. Copper was 18 years old. In addition, he had severe injuries. The back of Copper's foot had been chopped off when he had stepped beneath the blades of some farm equipment; his injury required lots of tender care and special shoes—not a confined and inattentive setting. While Mary Beth had many other more pressing problems at the time, she felt compelled to step in and help Copper.

Photo and story submitted by Mary Beth Hall

She borrowed a horse trailer and drove 100 miles to pick up the horse. His coat was dull, his mane and tail were short, and he had no barn or shelter to live in. Mary Beth loaded him into the trailer and brought him to her tiny farm.

Despite the injury to Copper's foot, vets were able to repair much of the damage. Copper remains a little short strided on the foot, but Mary Beth claims that since his medical attention, he's become a wonderful riding companion.

Copper is not Mary Beth's only horse; she also boards Patrick, a young Arabian who suffered from a severe fear of thunderstorms.

During storms, the horse would panic, run outside, and act uncontrollably. Fearing Patrick could be struck by lightning during his episodes, Mary Beth kept a close eye on the weather and would lock him in a stall before a storm started. Unfortunately, unexpected storms would roll in when Mary Beth wasn't home, and she worried constantly about Patrick's safety.

One day after Copper had joined the family, a storm was brewing, and Mary Beth ran out to the barn. She was surprised that Patrick was not pacing outside. She stepped into the barn and found Copper standing in the doorway. Every time Patrick tried to dash to the door, Copper would fire a kick in his direction. Mary Beth wondered why Copper would try to kick his buddy. Then she realized that Copper was teaching Patrick to stay in the barn during storms. From that point on, Patrick has learned to relax calmly inside the barn during the most dramatic of thunder and lightning storms. Mary Beth can now also relax!

Besides being Storm Protector, Copper is now the neighborhood kids' horse. He's safely carried most of the children in the neighborhood, plus all Mary Beth's friends' kids. All have enjoyed a ride and the view of nature from the back of a beautiful, gentle 1,200-pound horse.

Toffee and Arnie were both rescued by Tina, and disprove the rumors that cats and dogs can't get along.

Photo submitted by Tina Steele

Claudia and her husband were out for a run when they spotted some men dumping a litter of six Lab-mix puppies. Claudia rescued the puppies, and she and her husband found homes for all but one, who they chose to keep.

Photo submitted by Claudia Zulejkic

Nine-year old Faith desperately wanted a cat. Her father found Twinkle and suggested to Faith that she adopt her. Faith readily agreed, and she and Twinkle enjoy each other's companionship enormously.

Photo submitted by Faith Juchum

Charlynn and her husband had one poodle, Maggie, and decided to adopt another one. They began a search on Petfinder.com. There they found the perfect companion in Hershey, Pennsylvania, and named their new family member Sweet Hershey Kisses.

Photo submitted by Charlynn Lockard

Mary was volunteering at a shelter when a woman brought in two four-month old Australian Shepherd puppies. One puppy climbed into Mary's lap, and Mary took the puppy, Loki, home that night. Even though Loki is blind and deaf, he doesn't seem to know he's handicapped. He greets each day with joy and eagerness.

Photo submitted by Mary Scioscia

Liberty had been used as a "breeder" and then dumped in the park with no food or water. Monique rescued her, and after Liberty regained her weight and health, Monique took in a foster puppy. Liberty played with the puppy, teaching her how to be a wonderful, loving, and loyal companion.

Photo submitted by Monique Laracuente

After the loss of their previous pet, Camille avoided going to her empty home. To ease her grief, she went to Petfinder.com and saw Bailey Boo, a Lab/Rottweiler cross, who she brought home. Despite an abusive past, Bailey Boo is now a healthy, 80-pound happy girl with a shining smile and a beautiful red coat.

Photo submitted by Camille Bowlin

Camden had been brought to a shelter as a stray, been adopted, and then returned to the shelter. Carmen met him and was smitten, adopting him that day. Later, she adopted another rescue dog, Abby, as a companion.

Photo submitted by Carmen Hoyme

Nathaniel found traces of cat paws in the snow, and after finding the cat, tried to bring her indoors. She refused. With diligence and patience, Nathaniel eventually made friends with the cat, Isabella, and was able to help her when she gave birth to a litter of two kittens.

Photo submitted by Nathaniel Darling

On Traci's birthday, she found herself at the local SCPA, which is where she met Kali (left). When Traci visited Kali in her kennel, Kali climbed up in Traci's lap and started licking her face. Kali joins Traci's other rescue dog, Niki, and another small friend.

Photo submitted by Traci Jones

After losing her dog, Sharron thought she wasn't ready for a new dog, but she and her mother visited Doggie Daze in a local park. Despite her reservations, Sharon took a look at the dogs and immediately fell for Patches. Now Patches is right at home with his feline "sibling."

Photo submitted by Sharron Miles

Heroic Dog Saves Family from Fire

Jennifer was looking to adopt a rescued animal, particularly a German Shepherd Dog, because she had recently lost her beloved German Shepherd Sassy. Jennifer searched Petfinder.com and found Lucy at a no-kill shelter, Quincy Humane Society, about a 90-minute drive from her home.

Jennifer and her daughter Miranda drove to the shelter, where they found Lucy, but the dog didn't look as Jennifer had expected. Unlike a classic German Shepherd, Lucy was skinny and had huge ears. After meeting Lucy, Jennifer and her daughter decided to look at other dogs. As Jennifer and Miranda walked down the aisle to meet the other animals, Lucy barked wildly. They returned to Lucy and took her outside to play. She wasn't the prettiest German Shepherd, but her winning personality quickly won over Jennifer and Miranda. They adopted her and brought her home.

Lucy and Jennifer quickly bonded. Jennifer enjoyed the dog's exuberance and goofy behavior. Lucy was quick to learn and enjoyed playing with Miranda and Miranda's friends. Then came the miracle.

Photo and story submitted by Jennifer Gorsuch

In March 2006, the family retreated to bed, but around 1 a.m., Lucy began jumping on Jennifer. She barked in Jennifer's face and threw a fuss until Jennifer got out of bed. As Jennifer walked down the steps, she smelled something. She immediately put Lucy and her other pets outside and woke up her daughter and husband.

The sump pump, located under the room where Miranda sleeps, had caught on fire. Smoke damage permeated the basement and the first floor of the home before the fire was extinguished. Luckily the fire was caught before it could cause structural damage to the home or injury to anyone in the house.

Since that night, Lucy was named PetsMart Charities Adopted Dog Hero, ASPCA Dog of the Year, and Illinois Veterinary Association Dog of the Year. She has also been featured in several articles applauding her miraculous act of courage.

The great love Lucy showed proved to Jennifer that she was a miracle dog, saving her house and her family. Jennifer says "Saving just one dog did not change the world, but my world is changed because of that one dog."

Denise and her husband joined the San Clemente–Dana Point Animal Shelter in San Clemente, California, as volunteer dog walkers. This is where she met Jenna, a Beagle/Lab mix who had been abandoned and brought to the shelter.

Photo submitted by Denise Gee

5 The Miracle Meeting

When many people think of bringing a pet into their family, they expect the first meeting to occur at the home of a well-researched breeder, or even through a friend finding himself unexpectedly with a litter of puppies. Sometimes, however, fate takes a hand in the matching up of a pet and pet parent, and the magical moment happens when it's least expected.

Perhaps a homeless kitten shows up on your doorstep when you most need a friend. Or a friend might call and ask if you can help rescue an abandoned dog. We've read some heartbreaking and uplifting stories of pets finding their parents in the most unexpected places. We've read of a police officer bringing a lost cat to a home he knew was friendly to cats. We've read of a homeless dog jumping into the arms of a corner-store shopper, locking eyes, and securing his place in his new home. As we've laughed and cried over the stories you submitted, it's become more and more clear that miracles happen every day, and pets and owners destined for each other will eventually connect.

And the miracles don't stop there. Once a rescued pet finds his forever family, the mutual benefits continue, with the pet and pet parent teaching each other and learning from each other. Every day with a beloved pet is a gift, and perhaps that gift is more precious when it seems that so little—an on-time flight, a decision not to circle back to check on a wandering cat, a trip to a different city—could have kept two so meant for each other from meeting.

And it's not just the pets and pet parents who are changed by their relationship; those around them also reap rewards. Pets can teach others to trust and believe again; they can teach others spunk and determination; and they can inspire others to try harder to enjoy the small miracles and joys of everyday life.

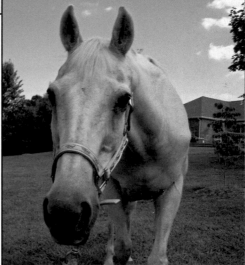

Tuesday looked high and low for a horse for her daughters. She discovered Oliver only 30 minutes from her house. Despite living with a terminal illness, he remains an upbeat and caring member of the family.

Photo submitted by Tuesday Tynan

When Megan saw Sebastian, he broke her heart, and she knew she wouldn't be going home without him.

Photo submitted by Megan Galey

Sophie was the runt of the litter and abandoned by her mother. Dennis picked up this little ball of fur, gave her a home, and nursed her back to health.

Photo submitted by Dennis Pastian

Teddy had a rough start. Found by the side of the road on Christmas Eve, he was picked up and taken to a vet. After the vet took care of the physical problems, Sandra, who owns several cats, took Teddy into her home and heart.

Photo submitted by Sandra Wittman

Three-Legged Dog Becomes Miracle Athlete

Pet parent Troy Kerstetter believes that everyone deserves a second chance, and he lives this philosophy. While working at a local Humane Society, Troy learned of several puppies who were found abandoned in a motel in Bend, Oregon. Troy arranged for the dogs, including a female named Maty, to be placed in foster homes and readied for adoption. During that time, the puppies were exposed to Parvovirus and had to be quarantined.

During the time in quarantine, Maty became lame, and a vet diagnosed a fracture that required expensive surgery. Maty spent the weekend before her surgery at Troy's home, and it became apparent to Troy that the dog *didn't* have a broken leg. He was right; she actually had an infection that affected her tendons and ligaments. As a result of the infection, Maty had to have her left rear leg amputated when she was about seven weeks old. She lived in the resident therapy puppy home until she was seven months old. In the therapy home, Maty received some special training and was taken out for pet visits to schools, local senior care and Alzheimer facilities, and local hospitals.

Eventually the therapy center where Maty was staying became too crowded, and Troy was asked to consider adopting the dog. Troy and his family not only welcomed Maty with open arms, but they began training her to compete in the Skyhoundz Disc Dog World Championships. The *Atlanta Journal–Constitution* ran an article about

Photo and story submitted by Troy Kerstetter

Maty, the first three-legged dog to participate in the competition. Maty competes in the Sport Division distance and accuracy, which occurs on the second day of the two-day event.

At the event one of the organizers arranged for Troy and his family to meet a special guest. A little girl named Sushma and her grandmother had read the article about Maty and traveled to see this special dog. As Troy and Maty approached their fans, they noticed that nine-year old Sushma was missing a limb. Maty quickly welcomed her, gave her the disc, and nudged her, hoping to get her to throw it.

But Sushma had other challenges; she was also missing the extremities of both arms. Troy and the group found an open area and demonstrated Maty's skills—how she could spin, weave through legs, and jump like a four-legged dog. Maty continued giving her disc to Sushma to throw until finally she grasped the disc, twisted her body, and gave a good throw. Maty returned the disc, and a special friendship was formed.

Sushma emailed her thanks for a special day. Her grandmother added that Sushma had just recently arrived in the U.S. and this was the first time she had laughed and had a good time. For all the smiles that Maty brings to people of all ages, the joy of Sushma will be the one Troy and his family will treasure forever.

A bout of insomnia led Shelly to adopt Ike; she started browsing Petfinder.com and came across the picture of her new friend. Ike became part of her family the next day.

Photo submitted by Shelly Hawes-Smith

Patricia was in her car when she spotted Cooper. Fearful she would hit the dog, she was looking around the car as she pulled out to be sure he was safe. That's when he jumped into the passenger seat window and into her heart.

Photo submitted by Patricia Kirchner

A neighbor found Veronica and asked Yvette whether the dog belonged to her. Needless to say, she wasn't her pet, but she quickly became one of the family.

Photo submitted by Yvette Fitzjarrald

Cooper traveled from a high-kill center in Ohio to a shelter in Pennsylvania, which was said to be his "last stop" before being put down. Elizabeth adopted him in the nick of time, and the two now live the good life in New York City.

Photo submitted by Elizabeth Kim

Stacey had no intention of adopting a pet until she attended an SPCA fair and fell in love with Angelle. Perfect timing!

Photo submitted by Stacey Warnke

Lucky Displays Many Amusing Talents

While traveling in Des Moines, Iowa, Carmena Cataldo and her husband saw a cat lying on the highway. They initially drove past him, but then quickly decided at the next exit to turn around and pick him up. Stopping the car, they feared that he was dead. As Carmena approached the little cat, however, he raised his head. She picked him up, took him home, and nursed him back to health. The Cataldos appropriately named their new companion Lucky.

And what a special cat Lucky has turned out to be! The Cataldos call him the "cat-dog." He retrieves toys over and over until he collapses from running so much. He is also very vocal and "talks" constantly. He wakes up Carmena's husband by picking up his toy, laying it across the husband's feet, and carefully scratching his feet. He also loves to wrestle with the other cats in the home, sneakily getting up and about so that he can settle, undisturbed, into his favorite sleeping spot.

Lucky's funniest talent, the family agrees, is his perfect imitation of the RCA dog. As the family watches TV, Lucky sits in front of the screen and watches, as well. If an animal appears on-screen, he goes to the TV and tries to touch the animal in an attempt to add another friend to his ever-growing list.

Carmena is thankful for the chance meeting that ended with a great family friend, stating, "Although his name is Lucky, I believe we are truly the lucky ones."

Photo and story submitted by Carmena Cataldo

From horrible living conditions and lack of attention and riding, Trigger, a miniature stallion, was rescued by Audra. Now he happily enjoys being ridden by children.

Photo submitted by Audra Knapp

Shana was looking for a "horse dog" and found Tana on a local shelter's website. Now Tana follows Shana when she feeds her horse.

Photo submitted by Shana Westbrook

Seeking a companion for her other cat, Melissa looked first at the local shelter where she works, and found Skipper, a lovely, deaf cat needing a home. His deafness doesn't seem to affect his zest for life: Skipper is a curious, playful, and talented cat.

Photo submitted by Melissa Landon

Charles picked up Purdy at an animal shelter in England; when his family moved to the United States, Purdy, a regular jet-setter, came along.

Photo submitted by Charles Matthews

Hope survived Hurricane Katrina and was found by a search and rescue team that included Ronald. Ronald's intention was to find a home for the dog, which he did: His!

Photo submitted by Ronald Desnoyers

Persistence Pays off for Rescued Horse

Desi was described as "the horse nobody wanted." She was given away when she was seven years old, then sold for $1, and then found and rescued by her pet parent Lisa Noto.

Desi was a "nightmare" when she first came to Lisa. She was anxious; she bucked, reared, and spun around in her stall. Lisa tried moving her from stall to stall until she found one that Desi finally settled down in, but the horse would not stand still. She'd buck, rear, hold up her feet—even balance on two feet! She reacted the same way when she was placed in the pasture: buck, rear, scream, and run along the fence line. In less-than-complimentary horse terms, she was "buddy sour, barn sour, and herd bound." She didn't want her face touched and was clearly psychologically damaged from her years of neglect.

Lisa contacted the two pervious owners who said they'd take Desi back, but added that in doing so they would put her down. Lisa couldn't abide this option so she read numerous books on natural/holistic horsemanship, watched videos and TV specials on horses, and researched her options online. She also solicited outside help. Her painstaking, hard work paid off and the horse made a miraculous transformation.

Fourteen months later Desi is a truly amazing horse. She no longer bucks or rears, she stands perfectly still to tie, and she even falls asleep when she is being groomed. She understands all her cues and is a joy to ride.

Desi didn't need to be put down; she needed someone to love her and make her feel safe. Lisa is very glad that she listened to her heart instead of outside influences when it came to the care of this special horse.

Photo and story submitted by Lisa Noto

When the Marks' home burned down, Max, who had just been adopted from a shelter, survived the fire by jumping through a glass window to escape the burning building.

Photo submitted by Katie Marks

When Sara arrived at a local shelter, all but one of the cats were meowing loudly, with one squeaking. Sara found the squeaking cat, and when the shelter staff released the kitten from her cage, the tiny kitten ran straight to Sara and sat on her shoulder. Sara took the kitten, who she named Annie Duke, home that day.

*Photo submitted by
Sara Blackwood*

Angela believes in getting any pet from a shelter, so when her local pet store hosted an adoption day, Angela visited and picked up Lola, who has proven to be both smart *and* beautiful.

*Photo submitted by
Angela Edmonds*

While in Grenada, Melissa worked as a volunteer for the local shelter. Someone brought in Lulu, who was in poor shape. Melissa decided the dog would get more attention in a home than a shelter, so she adopted Lulu!

Photo submitted by Melissa Bahleda

Nancy volunteers at the local shelter and one day met Diamond, who suffered from multiple problems. The shelter worked on Diamond's physical problems, and Nancy would visit the cat working on her social skills. One day Nancy simply decided to adopt Diamond, and brought her home to join her two other rescued cats.

Photo submitted by Nancy McCollum

From Central Park to the Good Life

"It was a dark and stormy night" is how this story starts. One evening a litter of just-born kittens were put in a box and left in New York City's Central Park. The defenseless kittens faced an uncertain future, but were saved through the efforts of a dedicated group of people.

The next morning, the park Zone Gardener was making his rounds in Shakespeare's Garden and found the box. Picking up what he believed was trash, the gardener was surprised to hear a tiny "meow." Instead of the refuse he expected, he found four tiny kittens. Thus began the kittens' journey to salvation.

The gardener immediately took the kittens to Belvedere Castle in the Park where the Central Park Conservancy Staff and Park Rangers spent the rest of the day trying to keep them warm. At the close of the day, one of the Rangers took all four kittens home; with the help of her children, the little kittens were bottle fed and cared for.

Photo and story submitted by Nathan Smith

Another resident in the Ranger's building was a vet and a self-proclaimed "cat" person, so the apartment building came together to keep the kittens alive and healthy. The story of the saved cats made its way around the building, and soon all of the kittens found good homes.

One adoptive pet parent, Nathan Smith, agreed to take one of the cats even though his wife is allergic to felines. Together, they named the cat Zoey. Since adopting Zoey, Nathan and his wife have taught her to purr, play tag, come when called, and play catch. Zoey also has an abnormal obsession with boxes. In fact, her pet parents often leave boxes around the house randomly for Zoey to play with. They know that when they look in the box, they'll find Zoey, just as that caring gardener did one stormy morning in Central Park.

Someone placed a tiny abused cat in a dumpster, and while most ignored the meowing, Jennifer didn't. Her husband put out food. They put up flyers and looked into Petfinder.com, but no one took any interest in this poor abandoned cat, so she named him Motley and brought him home.

Photo submitted by Jennifer Stevens

When Carly visited the Humane Society, one dog in particular barked and barked until she locked eyes with Carly. Carly knew then that Molly was the dog for her.

Photo submitted by Carly Kendall

Bart was rescued where he lived—in a cemetery. People and animal shelter volunteers tried to capture him, but he proved elusive. They finally captured him while he was sleeping. He initially stayed in a foster home until Patricia adopted him.

Photo submitted by Patricia Mason

Mike was browsing the fish in a pet store; that particular day the local shelter was hosting an adoption day. Out of nowhere, Harley ran into Mike's arms, bit his finger, and held on tight. How could Mike resist?

Photo submitted by Mike Crouse

Christena brought her son to the house of a friend who had several small parrots. Her son immediately was smitten by Aiko and begged his mom and the owner to take the parrot home. The mutual love between the parrot and boy was evident, so her son won out. They bought a cage and took Aiko home.

Photo submitted by
Christena Snowden

Smiley was placed in rescue and spent a lot of time at the local kennel waiting for a foster home when Sanya decided to foster him. After they were separated briefly, Sanya realized she could not part with him again, so she adopted him.

Photo submitted by
Sanya Dunn

Therapy Dog's Work Honors Little Emily

Kathleen Caganek has always known the importance of rescuing animals; her mother rescued animals and instilled in Kathleen the importance of caring for those who are discarded and unwanted, stressing that every living thing has value.

While fostering two dogs, Kathleen's mother received a call from a woman who desperately wanted to adopt one of the dogs. The caller's five-year old daughter, Emily, was dying of cancer. The little girl's biggest wish was to have her own puppy to care for; unfortunately, the cost of her continued treatment left no money for extras like the adoption fee for a puppy.

Immediately the rescue group agreed to conduct the adoption without a fee. Kathleen began obedience training the calmer of her two foster puppies, and within a short time, the puppy came to live with Emily and her mom.

Within weeks of seeing her wish for a puppy granted, Emily lost her fight with cancer. At that moment Kathleen made a promise to herself: She would train the other pup to become a therapy dog in honor of Emily. This dog, named Tally, earned several training certificates including her Canine Good Citizen. She is also in the B.A.R.K.-9 program; in this program, Tally visits libraries twice a week. While at the library, Tally sits quietly while children read to her. Many children have difficulty reading or are intimidated to read in front of others, but are comfortable reading to a loving, furry listener.

Tally and Kathleen love their jobs, and in Emily's memory they are giving of themselves to young children.

Photo and story submitted by Kathleen Caganek

Abby volunteered at the local Boxer
Rescue. When a friend called and said a
reverse brindle Boxer had been rescued,
she rushed over to pick him up. Remington
is not only a loving companion, he's also
Abby's inspiration for rescue. His spirit and
energy have allowed her to foster over 20
boxers with Legacy Boxer Rescue in the last
two years.

Photo submitted by Abby Paulson

6 New Beginnings

Welcoming a pet into your home and heart can provide not only a new beginning for the pet, but for you as well. The new furry or feathered friend can begin to trust again, as he settles into a home where he is loved, fed, secure, and well cared for. He may learn how to play and enjoy life. He even may develop a deep loyalty and skills that he may use to protect his family from harm.

Pets may make bonds with other pets—friends they can romp and tussle with. They may mentor other pets, teaching them socialization skills, or they may be mentored and taught how to behave in a home setting. Mostly, pets learn the special bond of being part of a family.

Some pets go beyond just learning the security of a happy home; these pets develop unknown talents or personality traits. They may become therapy dogs visiting hospitals and nursing homes, bringing joy to the patients and residents at these sites. They may master special skills, competing in special events such as agility and flyball.

Likewise, bonding with a new pet can give you a new lease on life, as well. Taking care of a pet whose past was spotty can give you a sense of responsibility and purpose. Witnessing a pet rebound from physical and mental abuse can help you find the strength to deal with other challenges in your life. Pets can help people struggling with depression or other illness just by providing their unconditional love. Pets are not judgmental; they are compassionate, understanding companions, and often they are the needed balm during times of grief, illness, sadness, heartbreak, or other problems.

So when you consider new beginnings, think not only of the pet and his or her new beginning or those that the pet may help, but also the new beginning for you or a family member. Pets can truly transform your life.

Jacqueline spied Thomas, whose elderly owner had recently passed away, at a pet store hosting a rescue agency. It was love at first sight.

Photo submitted by Jacqueline Smith

Missy Mae was a tough cat to place—grumpy and full of attitude. Pepper gave her a home, and now she has love to shower on others, like this lucky kitten!

Photo submitted by Pepper Mintz

Jennifer adopted Gracie after hearing of her story: Gracie had been hit by a car in southern Texas and was rescued and eventually brought to Weimaraner Rescue. Gracie is now training to be a Therapy Dog.

Photo submitted by Jennifer Walz

"Fun! Energetic! Friendly!" is how pet parent Kimberly describes Mochaccino, who she adopted at 10 weeks from the North Shore Animal League. This talented dog knows American Sign Language.

Photo submitted by Kimberly Mockler

This adorable household of Yorkies is made up of Bruno, Gizmo, and Emmett. Bruno and Emmett are rescued pets.

Photo submitted by Karli Meyer

Miss Fancy Pants was going to be sold to a Tiger Rescue site to be used as food but was rescued by Leslie. Since her rescue, Miss Fancy Pants is clearly enjoying her new life: She's putting on weight, and her coat is becoming smooth and sleek.

Photo submitted by Leslie Newberry

Maggie noticed a cat and her kittens on her front yard; she tried to take them to the shelter where Maggie volunteers. The mother and all the kittens but one tabby took off running. Tommie, the little tabby, ran to Maggie, who gave him a home.

Photo submitted by Maggie Wetzel

Jamie worked at a camp during summers that took left-over animals from a pet store, destroying the animals at the end of the season. Jamie rescued Honeybell from a plan to feed her to a snake. While Honeybell went through a tough transition in her new home, she knew she was safe with Jamie and learned to trust again.

Photo submitted by Jamie Nowak

From Adopted Dog to World Flyball Champion

Kate Bailey set out with a particular dog in mind. She knew that many purebred dogs are abandoned or surrendered, so she researched this option. She also knew that her busy, unpredictable schedule wasn't conducive to taking on a puppy. Her research led her to Knoxville, Tennessee, where many pets rescued from Katrina were being housed. It was in Knoxville that Kate met Emma, a Golden Retriever.

Emma turned out to be the perfect dog for Kate. From her first obedience class, it was clear that she would be a star. When Emma was initially rescued, she barely understood the command "Sit," but Kate was able to teach her new commands in minutes. She continued through other classes, passing with excellent results.

That April, Kate and Emma found their true love: flyball. Flyball is a relay race that involves four dogs. Each dog in turn leaps over four jumps, retrieves a ball off a spring-loaded box, and then returns over the jumps; then the next dog on the team does the same.

Emma and Kate are members of the Chattanooga Chomp Flyball Club and compete in tournaments all over the southeast. While Border Collies are the ideal flyball competitors, some Golden Retrievers do participate, and Emma has excelled at the sport. She's a natural, and at her first tournament, Emma's team took first place both days.

In the singles races, though, Emma became a superstar. In this competition, dogs race alone, ranked by time. When Emma first raced the singles, the fastest Golden Retriever time for the race was 4.623 seconds. In her first race, Emma set a new record with a time of 4.414 seconds, making her the fastest Golden Retriever registered with United Flyball (U-FLI).

Emma's not just a speedy, sports-talented dog. She also has her Canine Good Citizen and Therapy Dog International titles. Kate is most excited about her Therapy Dog title because now Emma can share her wonderful personality with others.

Photo and story submitted by Kate Bailey

Cynthia visited Alligator Alley, which runs an iguana rescue. There she came across Gwenie. Both Cynthia and her husband fell in love with the iguana and adopted her that day.

Photo submitted by Cynthia Groves

Laurie volunteers at her local rescue shelter and also fosters several animals. She knows that she can't keep every animal she fosters, but something about Arnie (left) touched her heart, and she brought him into her home.

Photo submitted by Laurie Benedict

Marie adopted Pee Wee, an elderly and hard-to-place dog, from a local shelter where she works. This photo of Pee Wee won second place in the Pets category of the International Photography Awards!

Photo submitted by Marie Staddon Dolphin

When Maria met Cocoa in a shelter, Cocoa was a quiet, calm puppy with eyes that spoke volumes. Fourteen years later, Cocoa still has a hypnotic gaze.

Photo submitted by Maria Buchert

As a wildlife rehabilitator, Mitzi received a rescue call about a fawn that had been hit by a car. Mitzi brought the fawn, Daisy, to her home for rehabilitation. During her recovery, Daisy made friends with Jeeves, a puppy given to Mitzi. Once Daisy recovered, she was reintroduced back into the wild.

Photo submitted by Mitzi Boles

Gracie was one of 14 dogs rescued from a puppy mill in Georgia. She had suffered many physical problems, as well as a broken spirit. Kimberly and her family worked to gain her trust and now she walks confidently with her tail in the air.

Photo submitted by Kimberly Mayers

Lacey had been terrorized by kids, given to another owner, turned over to the Michigan Humane Society, and then placed with a private rescue group, Top Dog Rescue. Lindsey and her family saw Lacey's picture, read her sad story on an online placement site, and decided to give her a new home.

Photo submitted by Lindsey Alpert

The Duchenes visited a local animal shelter "just to look." Once Chloe was in the play yard with the family, there was no resisting her charm. Within the hour they had completed the adoption paperwork, and Chloe came home with them the next day.

Photo submitted by Lisa Duchene

A New Career Courtesy of a Rescue Dog

Catherine Keenan and her husband have gotten all of their pets from shelters or rescues. At this point their household includes two dogs, Jake and Kizzy, and two cats, Bailey and Cleo. All four get along swimmingly. In fact, Bailey likes to rub his head along Jack's head and stick his nose in Jack's ear, and Jack, who has had some severe medical problems, lets both cats take care of him.

In December 2003, Jack was diagnosed with masticular myositis, an autoimmune disorder that causes the immune system to attack the muscles of mastication (chewing). As a result of the disease, Jack could open his mouth only about ¼ inch. Catherine consulted many specialists, but they all had nothing but medicine to offer.

Catherine was disappointed with the specialists' responses and felt there had to be help for Jack if she could just find it. She was heartened to find a vet who practiced alternative medicine, treating pets with both acupuncture and Chinese herbs.

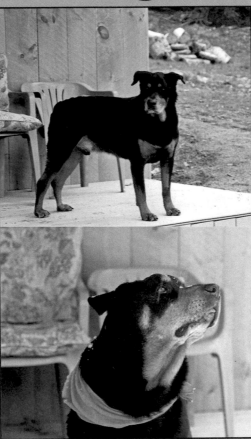

Photos and story submitted by Catherine Keenan

Catherine brought Jack to this specialist and discussed the treatment options available. At the first meeting the vet mentioned that she was a student at the New England School of Acupuncture.

When Catherine returned home, she looked up this school, and something clicked: Catherine knew immediately that this was what she wanted to do with her life. She has since graduated with a Master's of Acupuncture and Oriental Medicine and is now pursuing a second Master's degree in Pain Management from Tufts University. She would like to use her dual degrees to incorporate Oriental medicine into pediatric pain management services. She says, "I feel like this is what I was meant to do with my life, and I don't know if I would have found it without Jack."

Meanwhile, within six months of his treatments with acupuncture and herbs, Jack was weaned off all his medication and has not had a flare-up since.

Nineteen years ago Karen saved Rocky from being euthanized. Today he is a professional working turtle for Turtlesinger, Inc. (www.turtlesinger.com) and is the first and only turtle to be inducted into the New Jersey Animal Hall of Fame.

Photo submitted by Karen Buckley

In her search for a dog, Gabriella visited several websites. She saw Boss on the first day of her search and fell in love with his sweet face, but was afraid to take on a puppy. Eventually, Boss won her over, and he now enjoys hiking trips with his family.

Photo submitted by Gabriella Schiavino

All of Marsha's dogs—including DeeDee, Shylow, Nina, JC, and Nicki—have been adopted or given to Marsha.

Photo submitted by Marsha Hatfield

Iona was facing a lonely Christmas when neighbors dropped by with three kittens they'd rescued from a dump. Iona took them in and named them Mele, Kaliki, and Maka.

Photo submitted by Iona Ward

Bijoux is one of the lucky kitties who made it out of Louisiana after the Katrina disaster, and Ducky was adopted from a shelter to be a companion for Bijoux.

Photo submitted by Vencka Peterson

One morning a beautiful calico cat looked in Vivette's kitchen window; the cat had been thrown out by a neighbor for having litter after litter of kittens. Vivette enthusiastically took in the cat, who she named Pretty Pretty Princess Queen of the Universe Pet Me First.

Photo submitted by Vivette Ashen-Brenner

The Hurons went to the local animal shelter "only to look." But when Suzanne let Sasha out of her cage, the dog sat in her lap. Next thing she knew, Suzanne was scraping together enough coins to make the $25 adoption fee, and Sasha became part of the family.

Photo submitted by Suzanne Huron

Summer was rescued from a shelter in West Virginia, one with a high-kill rate; she was placed with HART, the Homeless Animals Rescue Team. From there she was placed in several foster homes until Laurel took her home for good.

Photo submitted by Laurel Vaccaro

Mary brought home Whisper, who she found in a field, and nursed her back to health. Miraculously, her son—who is allergic to cats—hasn't had an allergic reaction to Whisper!

Photo submitted by Mary Hagenston

Jayna adopted Jack as a kitten from a local no-kill shelter. Jack later was blessed with a canine sibling, Joey, who was given a home after being found wandering aimlessly in a parking lot.

Photo submitted by Jayna Thurman

Bentley Trains to Help Kids Become Literate

Amy Ondeyka wanted a dog and knew she wanted to adopt one from a shelter, so she began researching breed types on Petfinder.com. When she came across Bentley's face, she just knew she had to meet him. A unique mix of a Beagle, Bassett Hound, and a long-hair Daschund, Bentley is what Amy calls her "cut and paste" dog. When she met him in person, it was love at first sight.

Amy claims that Bentley's calm and loving personality

Photo and story submitted by Amy Ondeyka

doesn't reveal his past, which included abuse and neglect. In fact, she decided to share her wonderful dog with others; she knew he had the potential to bring joy into the lives of patients and residents of hospitals, nursing homes, and rehabilitation facilities. She started to research Animal Assisted Activities/Animal Assisted Therapy programs, better known as Therapy Dog programs.

When Amy came across information about the Delta Society, she knew she had found the perfect fit for Bentley. First he went through the training portion, fine-tuning his basic obedience skills.

Then he passed—and excelled in—the evaluation. After Bentley received his badge and vest in the mail, he and Amy were off to visit nursing homes and rehabilitation facilities. Amy says that she feels overwhelming joy when her rescued dog snuggles up to the wheelchair of an Alzheimers patient, and the patient remembers the dog's name. She's also moved at the smiles Bentley brings to AIDS patients and their families.

Amy and Bentley are looking to add to their charity work, and are also in the process of starting a Reading Education Assistance Dogs (R.E.A.D.) program at their local library. In this program, children improve their reading skills by reading to a therapy dog, who won't judge or interrupt them. Amy hopes Bentley will be sharing his love and understanding soon with children, as well.

"Bentley has excelled at everything I have ever asked of him," says Amy, "and he never fails to surprise me." She claims he will always be her hero.

The Beasleys were out walking their other two dogs. On the way home they pulled off at a dump and heard sounds coming from the bushes. Some investigation led to little Millie, a puppy, who immediately became part of the family!

Photo submitted by Amy Beasley

Cammy showed up on the Weeks' door step on Christmas and decided to make herself at home. Later, the family adopted another cat to be Cammy's companion.

Photo submitted by Stephanie Weeks

Jennifer and her husband met Moe at a local pet store that would help place rescued pets. She says of their first meeting, "He sat right down very nicely, closed his eyes as though in complete bliss, and then leaned in towards us. We were his."

Photo submitted by Jennifer Coon

Moving Past Katrina, Together

During Katrina, Candace lost everything—her husband and her house. When she was finally able to return to New Orleans, she lived with some good friends and their two dogs. In addition to the dogs, the friends were foster parents to animal victims of Katrina.

Photo and story submitted by Candace Clanton

To take her mind off her own situation, Candace decided to volunteer at the local shelter. Her friends encouraged her to consider becoming a foster or full-time parent to a Katrina victim dog. Candace didn't take the idea very seriously as she didn't have her own home at the time. But she jokingly said that she loved Rat Terriers, and if one were rescued, the shelter could call her.

The shelter manager lamented, "We *never* get breed-specific matches." Yet one week later, the rescue team at a shelter got a call that some dogs had been heard inside a collapsing house. When the rescue team arrived, a FEMA work crew informed them that a check had been performed near the house for gas lines in preparation for bulldozing this house. One of the workers heard dogs whining and whimpering as he crawled near the house looking for the gas line.

The work crew called Animal Rescue, and a rescuer crawled into the house and found a section where three dogs were trapped with no means of escape. Miraculously, those three dogs were comprised of two Miniature Doberman Pinschers and a Rat Terrier.

Two days later Candace got a call that her "specific request" had been granted. A brave Rat Terrier who had survived on the water pockets left from the flood and the boxes and jars of food in the house was waiting to have a better life with a new owner. And that owner would be Candace!

Candace and her Rat Terrier, who she named Bailey, have helped each other weather a terrible ordeal. Candace explains that Bailey is her "inspiration when I need to revitalize my determination and perseverance in the long-term effort we all are making to survive Katrina and get our lives back to normal here in the Big Easy."

Mourning the loss of her previous pet, Brilya asked her grandmother to take her to the local shelter. There Brilya picked out Vansey Boy. She had to nurse him back to health due to a case of kennel fever, but he recovered to become a happy and healthy companion.

Photo submitted by Brilya McCraney

Denise and her partner rescued this deaf Dalmation from being euthanized, and named him Alexander Bell in honor of Alexander Graham Bell, whose mother was deaf.

Photo submitted by Denise Tierney

Mary Kathryn knew she was ready to adopt another dog. She found Blossom on Petfinder.com, but was in the middle of completing her Master's degree, so was hesitant. Over spring break, she decided just to visit Blossom, and ended up taking him home.

Photo submitted by Mary Kathryn Back

When Neo was rescued, he was very ill and furless. The minute the Duncans saw "that bald little piglet" they knew that he was meant to be theirs.

Photo submitted by Brandy Duncan

Afterword

We hope you've been inspired and uplifted by these beautiful and poignant tributes to pets and their forever families. Reading these stories and looking at the gorgeous photos has moved us to tears and laughter—sometimes simultaneously!

If you're thinking of adding a friend to your family, do consider rescue. As the stories attest, so many wonderful pets are out there, waiting to give and receive love, and just need a chance to meet the right pet parent.

Following are some resources that will be helpful as you begin your journey to help a pet realize his or her own happy ending.

The American Society for the Prevention of Cruelty to Animals (ASPCA)

The ASPCA fights to ease the injustices animals face today and seeks to find safe, loving environments for all animals. The ASPCA website includes extensive health, training, and care information to help you best care for you new friend.

424 E. 92nd Street
New York, NY 10128-6804
212-876-7700
www.aspca.org

The Humane Society of the United States (HSUS)

HSUS is an animal protection organization that strives to be a voice for all animals, guarding them from anything that threatens their safety or happiness. You can adopt a pet through HSUS shelters throughout the country.

2100 L Street, NW
Washington, DC, 20037
202-452-1100
www.hsus.org

Find A Pet Online

Through this resource, you can find a pet in need of adoption, as well as locate veterinarians, breeders, trainers, groomers, and pet boarding facilities.

www.findapetonline.com

Next Day Pets

Next Day Pets enables prospective pet parents to find a dog, post dog listings, communicate with other animal enthusiasts, shop for pet supplies, and access a wealth of helpful information about the care of dogs.

www.nextdaypets.com

Pets4You

This extensive network is for animal lovers of all types. Through the Pets4U directory, you can find pets including cats, dogs, birds, reptiles, farm animals, and exotic pets.

www.pets4you.com

Petfinder.com

This well-known online resource provides an extensive database searchable by entered criteria (such as breed or geographical location). In addition, you'll find extensive information about pet care.

www.petfinder.com

PETS 911

This organization consolidates adoption, fostering, lost and found, volunteer, shelter/clinic, and health and training information in order to provide a single source of information.

888-PETS-911 (888-738-7911)
www.pets911.com

MAKE ADOPTION YOUR FIRST OPTION™

We hope you enjoy these heartwarming stories of pets who found forever homes. There are many more "hopeful tails" waiting in shelters for happy endings.

Here's how you can help:

- Adopt
- Volunteer
- Become a member

Learn more at www.aspca.org

The ASPCA was founded in 1866 as the first humane organization in North America, formed to alleviate the injustices animals faced. We continue to battle cruelty today; whether by saving a pet who has been accidentally poisoned, fighting to pass humane laws, rescuing animals from abuse, or sharing resources with shelters across the country. We continue to work toward the day in which no animal will live in pain or fear.

WE ARE THEIR VOICE.™